Perspectives
Living in Dangerous Places
What Are the Issues?

Series Consultant: Linda Hoyt

Flying Start
to Literacy®

Contents

Why do people live in dangerous places?

There are almost 800 active volcanoes in the world and a huge number of people – almost 20 per cent of the world's population – live in their danger zones. There are several million earthquakes a year. Many are not noticed – they are small or occur in remote areas – but some can be catastrophic. Every year, two million people are affected by earthquake activity. Fortunately, we now have the technology and the knowledge to monitor volcanic activity and to predict the probability of earthquakes.

People living in potentially dangerous places put their lives and their homes at risk. How does living in a dangerous place affect their day-to-day lives? How can they protect themselves?

Living above the boiling Earth

It smells like rotten eggs and the ground is unstable, yet people choose to live in this thermal zone. In this article, Gail Jarrow tells us how New Zealanders use the features of the thermal zone to their advantage.

Why do people choose to live in this strange, unstable environment?

You know immediately that something strange is going on in the city of Rotorua, New Zealand. The air smells like rotten eggs. Plumes of steam rise from road drains. Peculiar crusts of yellow, white and red cover the rocks. Mud puddles bubble. Rocks burn your hands. The ground vibrates as a hissing geyser spews hot water 30 metres into the air. These areas are fenced off.

New Zealand is part of the Ring of Fire, a circle of volcanoes and earthquake-prone areas that surround the Pacific Ocean. Underneath Rotorua lies a huge reservoir of steam and hot water heated by molten rock. The steam escapes into the air through cracks in the rocks. Scalding hot water rises to the surface through openings in the ground, forming hundreds of hot springs and geysers throughout the city.

Minerals in the boiling water coat the ground near the hot springs and geysers with different colours – white from silica, red from iron, yellow from sulfur. The sulfur fumes tarnish silver and corrode electronic equipment such as televisions and computers. No wonder the city's nickname is "Rotten-rua"!

Different mineral colours of Rotorua's hot springs

Rotorua may not sound like the ideal place to live, but people who make their homes in the thermal zone have adapted well. The first settlers, the Māori, arrived 600 years ago and built villages around the hot springs. They considered the thermal areas sacred treasures and sources of spiritual and physical comfort.

The Māori used the hot water to wash and keep warm. They cooked their food by placing flax baskets full of meat and vegetables into steaming pools. Today, Māori in traditional villages still use the geothermal heat in the same way their ancestors did.

Māori women cook corn in a hot spring.

Other uses have also been found for the heat under the ground. Since the 1950s, electricity has been produced by drilling into the underground pockets of steam, then piping the steam to electricity-generating pumps where it turns turbines. Hot water from subterranean reservoirs heats many homes and businesses, and homeowners drill into the ground to obtain steam and hot water for washing, bathing and swimming.

But, in the 1980s, people noticed that increased extraction of steam and water from underground had reduced geyser activity. In order to preserve the unique thermal areas of Rotorua, the government closed many boreholes. Today, a regional council oversees the use of geothermal resources. It limits the number of new boreholes and prohibits drilling within 1.6 kilometres of Rotorua's major thermal areas – especially those considered sacred by the Māori.

The people of Rotorua have learnt to live with the dangers of the boiling Earth. The ground in the thermal areas of Rotorua is so thin and hot that the early Māori settlers had to bury their dead in aboveground tombs. Walkers in hot spots must stay on marked paths, or risk crashing through the thin ground and tumbling into a pool of boiling water. For safety, houses are not built in known thermal areas. But sometimes the steam and hot water break through the ground in unexpected places and a house must be abandoned. Imagine a geyser suddenly appearing in your front yard!

Visitors relax in a naturally heated pool near Rotorua.

Visitors from all over the world have been attracted to Rotorua's unusual landscape. Tourism has been an important business since 1838, when Māori first led expeditions of travellers to see the thermal areas. Many visitors come to soak in the hot springs, believing that the minerals in the water relieve aches and pains, relax muscles and soften the skin.

Over the last 150 years, several North Island volcanoes have spewed ash and created damaging mud and lava flows. No one knows when the next volcanic eruption or earthquake will occur. Until then, the earth under Rotorua keeps boiling.

The mountain came to me

Mount St. Helens is part of the Cascade Range in the state of Washington in the United States. Vijaya Khisty Bodach recalls the day Mount St. Helens erupted.

What are the risks of living near a volcano? Are there any rewards?

As a new arrival from India in 1979, I fell in love with the hills and valleys of the Palouse – a region in eastern Washington state. On my way to the Palouse, where my family would make its new home, I saw the majestic snowcapped Cascade Mountains through my aeroplane window. I thought about how nice it would be to go camping and hiking in those mountains the following summer. But before I had a chance to go, one mountain, Mount St. Helens, came to me.

Mount St. Helens before the eruption

13

On Sunday afternoon, 18 May 1980, as my sister and I played a game of cards instead of preparing for high school final exams, the sky darkened. I thought that it was a solar eclipse. We raced outside, thick black clouds of ash greeting us. Within minutes, we were covered by a fine blanket of grey powder. We went back in and turned our radio on to hear that Mount St. Helens had blown its top that morning! I didn't remember hearing the explosion or feeling the shock waves. I took off outside for a walk as ash rained down. I collected some in a spice bottle.

School got cancelled! But it was no vacation shovelling ash. We wore masks and hauled bags of it to the landfill for the next two weeks. I felt grateful that we were far enough away from the volcano (about 480 kilometres) to be blanketed by only a few centimetres of ash. The thought of being buried in a hot mud avalanche or mudflow was ghastly.

Ash from the Mount St. Helens eruption covered the streets of this town.

Grey permeated our lives those next few months. People complained of clogged air filters and corroded engines.

Yet, we ate the fattest, juiciest and sweetest tomatoes that summer. Our vegetable garden thrived year after year without the use of fertilisers. That fine ash is a natural fertiliser. Eastern Washington has periodically been dusted with it, creating soil perfect for growing wheat, lentils, peaches, cherries and grapes.

I didn't make it back to Mount St. Helens until ten years after its eruption. Its recovery amazed me. Mosquitoes buzzed around my head while I admired fireweed and lupines growing on the slopes. I saw elk roaming the barren Pumice Plain. The ghosts of once-tall trees stood eerily, sheltering small animals. I knew that a forest would again thrive when I saw young Douglas firs with brilliant green needles growing.

Last year, a new round of earthquakes and eruptions began at Mount St. Helens, and I took my children to see the smoking mountain.

The Christchurch earthquake, 2011

At 12.51 p.m. on Tuesday, 22 February 2011, a magnitude 6.3 earthquake caused severe damage in Christchurch, New Zealand, killing 185 people. Christchurch had experienced a stronger but less damaging earthquake in November 2010 – and yet another earthquake was to strike in 2016.

Anthony Smith was a visitor to Christchurch when the 2011 earthquake struck. In this article, he is left wondering how the people living in this city cope with what they have been through, and the threat that they still live with. What do you think?

Anthony Smith

It was around 12.50 in the afternoon. My sister-in-law Nicki had just driven my wife and me to the airport, and together we sat having coffee waiting for our boarding call.

Suddenly, I heard an extraordinary noise – the roar of a speeding freight train approaching us. The noise wave hit us, and everything around us rattled and swayed. I sat frozen, not knowing what was happening until Nicki said, "It's a quake! We have to get out of here!"

Outside the airport, crowds had gathered. The airport building was swaying because of severe aftershocks. There was no mobile phone reception and no power. The airport personnel told us that the airport was now closed for 24 hours while they assessed the damage. No one was injured, but everyone was shocked at the enormity of the event taking place all around us.

Nicki was worried about her husband. He worked on the other side of the city, and she had no way of knowing if he was okay. So the three of us headed off in the car to find him. The roads had flooded and the traffic lights were not working. Despite the damage and the chaos all around us, the traffic was orderly and drivers were polite to each other.

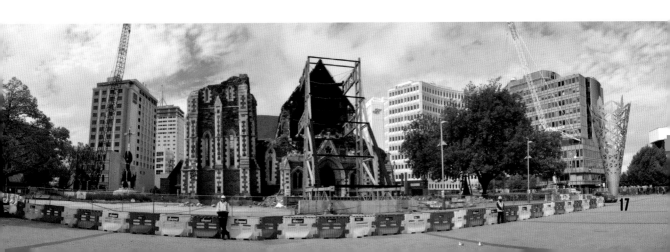

I'll never forget the people standing in the street, looking at their broken houses, comforting their crying children. I saw no injuries, just distress and great confusion. One block from Nicki's house, we had to abandon the car. The road had flooded because of liquefaction – water and sandy silt forced up out of the ground by the earthquake – and we could not see what was under the water.

We waded through knee-deep water to the front of Nicki's house. It was now about three o'clock in the afternoon. Nicki's husband had made it home safely, but his face told the grim news. The house was split in half. Mud covered the floors, furniture was thrown around and smashed glass was lying everywhere.

That night, we sheltered in the damaged house in the devastated Christchurch suburb. There was no power, no water and no way to communicate with the outside world. We collected water from where we could, even draining the toilet cistern. All night, we could feel the ground shake and we could hear water bubbling to the surface under the floorboards. The car radio was our only source of information – that's how we found out that the airport was likely to be open the following morning.

My wife and I decided to leave. It felt as if we were abandoning our relatives but it made sense – with the limited supplies of food and water, we would be a burden. Once again we were driven to the airport, this time through widespread scenes of utter destruction.

I was left wondering how the people of Christchurch coped – and indeed, still cope. Many people had to leave the city, as they had no accommodation. Some did not return. Large areas of land were declared unfit to be built on. Many buildings had to be demolished, others were able to be repaired. New and tighter building regulations, to withstand earthquakes, were developed. Quite a few people now keep emergency supplies on hand – just in case.

After the earthquake, research studies showed that people coped very well with the stress of the disaster. It was decided that their strong community spirit was a very important factor. It seems that for the people of Christchurch, their most powerful protection is their unshakable strength.

At home on the slopes of Mount Vesuvius

Mount Vesuvius, near Naples, Italy, is one of the world's most dangerous volcanoes. But about 600,000 people live in small towns at its base and they would be in grave danger if there was an eruption. The Italian government has offered assistance to help them relocate, but many people stay where they are. In this article, Claire Halliday explains why.

Why do people choose to live at the base of a volcano?
Should they move?

A deadly volcano

In 1944, the people in the Italian town of San Sebastiano – one of 18 towns built on the slopes of Mount Vesuvius – were forced to evacuate when the volcano erupted. The only building that survived the thick river of lava was an 18th century church. The rest of the town's buildings were burnt and crushed by the molten rock that poured through the streets. The people affected by the natural disaster rescued what they could from the rubble of their properties and started building again – this time with an extra thick layer of lava as their foundations!

In 1944, villagers watched as lava flowed down the main street of San Sebastiano.

During the past 17,000 years, Mount Vesuvius has experienced around 50 eruptions, including eight major eruptions. More than 16,000 people may have been killed. In 79 CE, a ferocious eruption destroyed the towns of Herculaneum and Pompeii. The site of Pompeii was discovered in 1748, and it is renowned as an important archaeological find.

Despite this history, almost three million people currently live in the surrounding areas of what is regarded as the world's most dangerous volcano – the only active volcano in mainland Europe.

Volcanic life – A ticking time bomb

From a laboratory in Naples – an Italian city near Mount Vesuvius – scientists use special equipment to monitor the temperature and movement inside the volcano's crater.

If warning signs indicate that the earth is fracturing, scientists predict that they will have about two weeks' notice before the eruption happens.

To help minimise the risks and the huge expense of a sudden evacuation by army, police and other local emergency service workers, the local government has offered families around 30,000 euros (approximately 45,000 dollars) to relocate out of the eruption zone.

Scientists monitor volcanic activity at a Naples observatory.

A farmer tends crops near Mount Vesuvius.

Benefits vs. risks

Despite the obvious potential danger, around 600,000 people
(20 per cent of the local population) live in what is known as the
"red zone" – a region around Mount Vesuvius that would take the full
impact of a major eruption.

There are many reasons why people choose to ignore the risk.
For some, it is loyalty to land that has been in their family for
generations. For others, it is profit from the tourism industry that
draws international visitors and provides a lucrative income for
business people who operate restaurants, cafes and hotels. The
volcanic soil is also very fertile – the perfect land for wineries and
farms to grow grapes and other varieties of fruits and vegetables.

But could the life they enjoy be wiped out forever if Mount Vesuvius
erupts again? For a large number of Italians in the region, it seems
they are willing to take the chance.

What is your opinion?: How to write a persuasive argument

1. State your opinion

Think about the issues related to your topic. What is your opinion?

2. Research

Research the information you need to support your opinion.

Related PERSPECTIVES book   Internet   Other sources

3. Make a plan

Introduction

How will you "hook" the reader?

State your opinion.

List reasons to support your opinion.

What persuasive devices will you use?

Reason 1
Support your reason with evidence and details.

Reason 2
Support your reason with evidence and details.

Reason 3
Support your reason with evidence and details.

Conclusion

Restate your opinion. Leave your reader with a strong message.

4. Publish

Publish your persuasive argument.

Use visuals to reinforce your opinion.